THE TALES SHE WROTE

OLUWABUKUNOLA AKINSANYA

THE TALES SHE WROTE

WRITTEN BY
OLUWABUKUNOLA AKINSANYA
oluwabukunolaakinsanya3369@gmail.com

Published by:
COMMUNE WRITERS INT'L
www.communewriters.com
+234 8139 260 389

Published in the Federal Republic of Nigeria

To Professor Biakolo Emevwo, I can't imagine the success of this book without you.

To Femi Ajayi, I appreciate all your advice.

THE GIRL I MET

As a child, I met a girl,
Till now, must say, still learning her ways.

She feels nothing but sees everything,
She possesses all but holds nothing.

She dwells in two worlds,
She lives in two worlds,
She dies in two worlds,
She is a shadow of her true form.

People are phantom that she passes through.
Her family is an unavoidable necessity.
Her concept of friendship is a relationship of
hypocrisy.

Love, pain, hate, and joy, are toys in her game box that
she play.
Her eyes are always in search of her next addiction.
She drowns in the deadly sins of the world as she can't
resist their seductions.
She eats her emotions,
She is only the reflection of who she wants you to see.

Her eyes are filled with nothing but emptiness.
Her days are dreams,
Her dreams are her reality.
Only when red floods from her cut do she remember
the real.

Never has she left my side,
And, how could she?
When she sticks to my body like glue.

WHAT A SAD LOVE

How do I explain this feeling to you?
This painful, sad love.
I love you even if it hurts,
I still love you when I hurt you.

How can you understand the way I show my love?
My eyes are always looking for you.
Your smile melts my heart,
Your eyes dig into me.

My words betray me.
I can't bear seeing you with him,
But I see your love for him is strong,
Even he knows my love for you is real.

Your voice breaks my violence,
I'm sorry I caused you pain,
But I am hurting him by hurting you.

How else do I not know how to love?
What a sad eye to watch you pass me by,
Forever I may have for you a sad love.

THE ONE I WANT TO LOVE

As I walk down this road with the street lights on,
I am searching for the one,
Whose eyes are filled with tears for me.

Time and time again we do this,
Because we refused to avoid an argument.
Your pride and my prejudice are the cause,
It is not a relationship where we should keep score,
It is not a perfect feeling.

A love that is far stronger than the past or present,
A love without a superior or subordinate,
A love that is neither a secret to hide from the world
nor painting to showcase,
A love that will go on after our lives.

Love with some days of crying and some days of
laughing,
Love with some days of craving and some days of
irritation.
This love is the connection of soul, body, and mind
flavored by emotions.

This love isn't perfect, but neither are we.

THE DIFFERENT SHADES OF HIM

When I talk with him, I feel at peace; I am with a good friend.
When I talk with him, I feel like I have a lover; there is desire and passion.
When I talk with him, I feel like I am a queen with a subject who's waiting for my commands.

When I talk with him, I feel like a student who's to be taught "love".
When I talk to him, I feel like I have a husband and a brother in one person.
When I talk to him, I am alive; I have a playmate and soul mate for life.

The different sides of him complement the different sides of me.
The different sides of me complement the different sides of him.
Without it all, he is incomplete.
Without it all, I am incomplete.

THE UNREQUITED LOVE

Let me tell you a love story,
A story of a special kind of love.

A selfish kind of love,

A love for one person alone.
"He is in love with her, she needs not to know"

A love that takes everything without asking.
"He knows her like no lover, her fears, her lies, her truth, and her strengths"

A love that has everything to win and nothing to lose.
"She could love him more but never less"

A selfless kind of love,

A love that is always waiting to give without expecting to receive.
"She tells him everything, she hides nothing from him, that's more than enough for him"

A love that never weakens in regret.
"His shoulder is always there for her to cry on wherever, whenever"

A love that can produce other kinds of love.
"He is a brother, confident, father, and friend"
He is a different kind of love; his love is unrequited.

WHAT IS EQUALITY

A man is a man,
A woman is a woman.
Equality is not a replacement for gender roles,
It is not colonialism of the sexes.

Equality should not be fought for,
It should have already been.
It is not a fight for supremacy,
It is the acceptance of the importance of balance.

It is the perception of a variety of beauty,
It is the assumption of a crafty conception of the
perfect woman.
It is a complementation of the opposite.
And this should be from both genders.

What is equality?
It is not something that should be discussed,
Or determined by the color of a person's skin.
It should have already been.

It is the embracing of different colors,
It is the understanding of varieties of languages and
cultures,

It is the appreciation of anybody and everybody for
who they are.

It is the picture of the world I want to see,
It is the picture of the world that should be.

MY CONFESSIONS

I must confess, first; that I am a growing child aiming to be an adult; then again, I may just be a stagnant adult aiming to be a child.

I must confess, I see the evil in everything; that is why I appreciate the good in anything.

I must confess, I dwell within the insanity of wisdom.

I must confess, the temptation is obsessed with me as I am with her.

I must confess that my mind is an endless dark hole.

I must confess, I do not often tell the truth.

I must confess, I am not quite sane.

I must confess, I am a poet with no poems, just stories, and tales.

I must confess, I have a lot of love and hate in me and most times, for the same people.

I must confess, I must repent, and I must relent.

I must confess, I love nothing, so I cherish everything.

I must confess, that this is not my first confession, and this confession will not change me.

THE AGONIES OF A CHILD OF THE WORLD

The world has lost her edge,
Her ability to evolve openly,
The truth is mummified by her duties and objectiveness.

She does not embrace the beauty of her breasts,
But instead, she houses children who have plucked out their own eyes.

She is a mother who cuddles her children until they choke.
She is a mother who feeds her children poison to heal them.

The world has lost her mind.
She sprinkles drops of the stupidity of her people,
Spraying violent insects into her tenant's homes.

She shares her wealth unevenly with her young ones; hence they kill each other.
She cuts down on her own body and chooses to be handicapped.
She brings in rapists to misuse her womanhood.

The world has lost her pride.
Her colors have faded,
Her body has gotten thinner,
Her natural beauty is painted with artificial hues.

A LETTER TO MY FATHER

There is a man I know,
A man that has robbed me of both my heart and my
love.

The only man for whom my tears endlessly flow,
The only man in my heart I cannot remove.

For his attention, I am always craving.
For his approval, I am always seeking.
A man I always seem to need but do not want,
But never will I beg.

I don't beg, for I am my father's daughter.
My pride is much bigger than my pains.

I guess strong is the blood that flows through my
veins.
I am the mirror of my mother and the frame of my
father.

I am like a coin; sometimes you get heads and
sometimes you get tails.
He always said "you may bleed, but you never knee"
"You must not plead and death is better if from a fight
you flee"

His disapproval, his disappointment, his disinterest, I take my daily dose.
The one I cannot escape,
My father, my judge, my jury, and my executioner.

LOST IN THE WORLD

I want to write a poem for my brother,
I want to sing a song for my friend.
I will tell a story like no other,
Of connections that will last to the end.

A man that mirrors Janus.
A man that confirms and contradicts my exceptions at once.
The importance of sacred ties that are woven by a twist of fate.
The choices and decisions that have affected us to date.

I want to write a poem for my brother,
I want to sing a song for my friend.

A man with depth like a pond,
A man with traits of the shades of gray,
A man who tastes like strawberries,
A man who shakes you with cold warmth,
A man who has unknowingly and unwillingly erupted many emotions in me.

THE PURPLE HEART

The purple heart is sad;
Her sadness makes her body ache.
The purple heart is a lying heart;
Her smiley face is fake.

The thoughts of cutting or splitting,
Burning or hanging,
Stabbing or drowning,
Swallowing or jumping.
The voices of blaming or hating,
Condemning or regretting,
Shaming or forgetting.

The purple heart is confused;
She is always on both sides of a coin.

The purple heart is wicked;
She is always making and breaking relationships like a
junkie with a fix.

The purple heart, yet in the world, is brighter than the
sun.
She is full of beauty.

ODE TO THE GIRL'S STORY

Let me tell you a story,
One filled with romance and horror,
One filled with wisdom and foolishness.

A story of a girl who does not want to grow up.
A story of a constantly changing protagonist and
antagonist.
One filled with different shades of lies and truth.

A story of love in all its forms.
A story of a girl whose only world is in her mind,
Where she is limited to the limitlessness of her
imagination.

She creates and destroys her friends at will,
And selects a different lover for whatever great
fantasy awaits her.
For only her mind belongs to her, and even that is to a
certain degree.
For her body is not her own, and her heart for another.

Today, the happy girl struggles more with her demons.
They hunt her, for she is weak now.
They taunt her, for she is delicate at this time.

The smile on her lips has become faker,
The words in her mouth were bitter,
The gesticulation of her movement was slower,
The thoughts in her heart darker.
The love in her heart, the one thing she kept pure, was
tainted by sadness and depression.

The sorrow in her heart knows no end,
They refuse to be appeased or changed,
They show their face at the slightest appearance of
happiness.
They cannot show her pain to others, but she cannot
hide it from herself.

Her perfect moments with her many lovers are her
only relief.
She tries to talk to herself to normalize,
But the wise words from her mouth do not reach her
foolish eyes.
She tries to talk herself to understanding the
objectivity of her knowledge,
Losing to the unstable tantrums of her heart.

This is the story of a young sad girl of today.

A WOMAN

A woman's mind is a mysterious place.
Many men try to understand it, and till today, it is defeat they face.
Many men have uncovered it, but find them peeling; another lay at every pace.

A lady's beauty, although fleeting, has been recorded to destroy kingdoms; just ask the people of Troy.
Many have submitted and are yet to submit to it.

A lover's fury is compared to the flames of hell.
Those on the receiving end of it never turn out well,
Those who have witnessed it always have a story to tell.

A mother's love is second only to the love of God.
For her child, no sacrifice too great to pay.
For her child, she could have done impossible things.

A wife's sacrifice is so great, even with ten lifetimes, many men in repayment, are found lacking.

A daughter's duty is never-ending.
Still, a female's body ever giving.

Her hands work and nurture her child and take care of
the home.
Her breast comforts and feeds her child, and still
pleasures her man.
Her legs and hips to accomplish multiple tasks
quickly.
Her back to comfort her child.
Her belly to carry her child.

LIFE'S WICKED WAYS

Life has made me a wanderer.
She answers my questions with more questions,
She mocks my little knowledge and makes fun of my reasoning,
She is an unfair dealer of fates and the greatest sadist of them all.

Like chess pawns, she moves and uses some.
While others are kings and queens, she is still bored again.
Where even the way to love needs to be put into a classification.
Where many people mock others living the lives they desire but are too afraid to live.

Where people choose to live in the comfort of fear than pain courage.
Where some decisions that require touch and hard actions will never be made.

Where mothers, nieces, sisters, wives, aunts, and grandmothers are now the major oppressors of fellow women.
Where old corrupt leaders grow older in their evil, while the young fight and die for their selfish agendas.

Where misguided religious institutions brainwash the public into the actions of destruction.

If there is little time anyway; if even seven times are not enough for me to make a difference,
I would rather remain a wanderer, just watching life play her wicked games with the world.

THE INTERNSHIP

A happy face and sad soul walk into an unknown place with a confused mind and an unwilling body.
A curious mind, childish character, and unsure spirit forced into an adventure-seeking knowledge and experience.

The trip was long for a short time, but short-lived for the longest time.
Some days were hard; my body betrayed my excitement.
Some days were lies; my duties were like two mountains on my back.
Some days were surreal; even the work was fun.

Faces are imprinted into my heart.
Many assumptions and presumptions, the light of knowledge chased out the dark.
The voices are recorded in my mind.

Surprising strengths and weaknesses I find.
Conversations out-valued gold.
In my life, little magic moments unfold.

For the first time, my heart wishes to commit, just a bit longer.
But we should end with a happy ending, so our story I fear, can't go any further.

CARELESS WORDS

"Hello, friend, don't worry, I know who you are"

"You will be there when I finally finish my race (and by this, I mean life's race)"
"You are there beside me when I fake my smile (I'm sure I am not the only one who does it)"
"You were there when I was always left alone (we played a lot)"

"You will be there when I succeed or fail (with me, you never know)"
"You are there when my thoughts are pure and not so pure (because no one is perfect)"
"You were there when thoughts of suicide crept into my head (they still do)"

"You will be there when I have my children (although I pray you won't)"
"You are there when I killed all those people (but only in my mind)"
"You were there when I did not break my heart (who can break something that's already shattered)"

"You will be there to question my decisions and indecisions in life (sometimes you nag a lot)"

"You are there when I requested and begged for your help (I know you heard, but you choose to remain silent)"
"You were there to force me to remain happy (as happy as I can be anyway)"

"You have been there when those people question my sanity (all because I tell them what you say)"
"You are there when those people whisper behind my back (not that doing it in front of me is better)"
"You will be there when they will call me crazy (I am not the one that told them not to speak for the voices in their heads)"

My friend, I told you I know who you are. "Goodbye, my friend".

A PLACE

There is a place I know.

I live in a country filled with traditions and swallow cultures.
Where there are listeners, there are watchers and there are complainers.
The holiest things that should be cherished are monitored.

The women live in a school in which there are rigid schedules.
The children understand the knowledge they digest.
The leaders are slaves to their greed and their envy.

The future of the people is in the hands of the unknown and uncaring.
The blood of the wrongly persecuted is what we bathe every day.
A place where you are taught the importance of lying.

THE CONFLICT BETWEEN THE DIFFERENT

Imagine a world without beautiful colors,
Where there was only black and white.

Imagine a world without wonder,
Where people were satisfied with what they had never
wanted more.

Imagine a world without imagination,
Where people could not look past what was
reasonable.

Imagine a world without varieties,
Where choices were strictly limited if there are at all.

A world where our minds are prisoners of limitation.
A world where our diversity was no longer as wide as
an ocean but was now as narrow as a pond.

For even flowers are admired for their different
shapes, sizes, and colors.
So then, why are we people condemned for not being
different, unique, and special in our appearances,
perceptions, and actions?

DEAR HEART

Dear heart, what fun you must be having, playing this game.
You fall out of love faster than you fall into it.
You ache so hard for the things you desire.
But you no longer care for it when you have it.

I fear and pity those in your web of capture.
Your fleeting love and attention are addictive and consuming.
That is why, even long after they have been abandoned, their love and desire for you is without measure.

What maze of confusion did you leave them in?
Your past lover's loyalty till now is never-ending.
What is this lust for the body you inhabit that keeps them?
Or was it your control of their minds that did them in?

Different types of prey but the same outcome,
Sometimes the chase is longer and other times shorter, but the catch is always sure.

The plague is hard, yes, I must confess; but whom I pity the most are their future or true lovers, who will

Dear Heart, what do I do with you?

be left in the shadow of the people these men used to
be.

ACID VICTIMS

The girl in the reflection is not me.
She is the girl he has tried to make me be.
She is timid and scared all the time,
Almost like my life is over while I am still in my prime.

Her skin color displaces several shades of brown and black, painted with a colorless liquid.
The makeup neither covers the inner scars nor the wounds outside.
She is either pitied, rejected or ignored by the spectators of her life.

She can still feel it all the time,
The burning feeling after the substance touched her face.
She would compare it to being burnt alive.

She can still smell it all the time,
The choking scent of blood, melting skin, and alcohol.
Now, even the thought of a hospital makes her sick.

She can still hear it all the time,
The sound of her screaming, the doctor giving instructions, and the well-wisher's words of comfort.

She sometimes wishes she could go deaf; at least then, she would not have to listen to them recite their practiced speeches,
While they question each other: "Who will marry her now?" "What did she do to provoke him to do this?"

MURDER OR SUICIDE?

The sound of birds, the blue sky, and the wet ground,
I would rather be anywhere else but on this burial ground.
All the people dressed in black here are hypocrites.
I woke up this morning wishing for the night to come quicker.
I am just confused, sometimes most may consider it a murder, others an accident, but to me, it was a suicide.

The family came to talk to a wall, oh they came aplenty. The man is winning every night in boxing and wrestling.
These scars have become more than makeup can patch.
The friends in the support system covered the marks and begged her to leave.

Then a new life comes to destroy another in nine months. The mother is weakened by the presence of her child.
The wife believes she needs to stay for the child.
The African woman dying for her social acceptance and approval.

Finally, the woman is dead, the husband is in jail, and the result is a motherless child.

So, if we were responsible for our decisions and choices, was it murder or suicide?

THE CHAINS WE CARRY

There are children in chains; the chains may differ in size and shade.
There are children in chains; these chains never leave them.
The chains, like air, cannot be seen or heard, but are surely there.

The innocent ones are yet to be aware of their chains.
For some, the chains tighten while for others it loosens.
The chains connect others with the same intensity that separates many.

Chains of culture carry the chains of choice of others.
Chains of gender carry the chains of nature.
Chains of race carry the chains of simply being a different creature.
Chains of exceptions carry the chains of things not done.
Chains of reputation, they carry the chains of those long gone.

There are people in chains even as they chain others.
Their number may decrease or increase, but they are never completely gone.

WHO IS SHE?

The cold wind slapped against her skin as she sat on
the school floor.
Even the rushing breeze could not put out the fire in
her.
Anyone would think she had a fever.
Her stomach had stabbing pain again.
This time it was not the smell of the fresh cow dung
from the pasture in front of her.

All her life she will be known by the names of two
men.
Their identities overshadow hers.

How is her mother responsible for her father's child?
If both genders are to marry, why is she the only one
prepared for it?
If science has proven that man is the sole determiner
of the gender of a child,
Why are women held accountable for it?

If she is not a wife, she has failed in life.
Does marriage mean success?
If she is not a mother, she is said to be incomplete.
Do a child or children complete a woman?

A girl is taught to kill her sexuality; still, he sees fit.
A boy is encouraged to exploit as he sees fit.
Is she in life just to be seen and not heard?
Is she to be used and controlled?

WHO IS A PERFECT WOMAN?

Who is the perfect woman?
What is her skin tone?

Who is the perfect woman?
What is her weight?
Is she fat, slim, or skinny?

Who is the perfect woman?
What is her body shape?
Is she a figure 8, figure 1, letter D, or letter B?

Who is the perfect woman?
What is her hair length?
Does she have long hair, short hair, or no hair at all?

Who is the perfect woman?
Is she quiet and submissive or outspoken and domineering, or a mix of both?
Is she a homemaker or a career woman, or both?

Who is the perfect woman?
Is she an equal partner in the relationship or a tool for your use alone?

Is she what you want or need in life?
Cause we all know that the last question does not have
a middle ground.

Who is the perfect woman?
Can she be a reality or is she just a fantasy that others
can't even reach up to?
Because any man who thinks he deserves his perfect
woman must first be her perfect man.

SCHOOL LIFE TODAY

This is a jungle where only the fittest survive.
You can see prey and their predators.
The strong hurt the weak,
The boys hunt the girls,
The lecturers hunt the students,
The rich hunt the poor.

This is a game center.
A place that can break or make lifelong connections.
This is a place where children want to get the pros of independence but avoid the cons.
The manner and players may change, but the game is the same across races, tribes, locations, and generations.

What do you do in school, many parents may have asked their children?

Here is your answer:
Some are trying to survive.

Some are building relationships stronger than academics.
Many are growing up and learning about life.

Some are enjoying the short window of carelessness before the responsibility of adulthood is forced on them.
Few are just carried away with new, expensive and pretty things.

A school is a place for learning.
Lessons of life,
Lessons of love,
Lessons of relationship,
Lessons of education.
All these lessons each require classes, assignments, tests, projects, and examinations.

THE EMPTINESS OF FEAR

See how powerful I am, I control the minds of many.

I am a frequent visitor to all (some people I never leave at all)

I am sometimes under the beds or closets of little children.

I am sometimes in the uncertainty of tomorrow.

I am sometimes in the inability to gain control.

I am sometimes expected after a long period of happiness.

I am sometimes reliving memories.

I am sometimes in the knowledge of the unavoidable death.

I am sometimes in the nothingness of darkness.

I am sometimes in the reason of the mind.

I am not biased in my selections of prey or the manner
of approach.

I am but a thought in your head.

You may delay my visits for a short while.
You may even reduce my duration of stay.
But I will surely come when you call for me.

EXPECTATIONS OF FAMILY

The child is born with a load on its back.
As the child's body grows, so does his load.

The child is the opportunity of its parent.
The burden of their failed dreams and bitter regrets on their shoulder.
The child is the answer to their prayers and is their fresh clay for molding.

The child's life is answerable to the owner that birthed him and raised him.
The child is meant to fulfill the desires of its family and continue its ways.

How dare the child dream a different dream than the one planned for him?
How dare the child wants a life apart from the one planned?
The child must run the race his father before him has ran.

The child was given life; it belongs to its father.

The child was given a name associated with responsibilities and conditions.
The child was given the education to become what was expected of him.

The child's purpose is to fulfill his parents' dreams; if he wants to fulfill his dreams, then when he is grown, he can have a child to do so.

SHAME ON THE WOMAN

Where shall I hide my face? I am a disgrace.
I have pleasured myself between my legs.
I have desired the pleasure of flesh before the wedding bells.
I have relations with men only for my physical hunger.
I have played under the sheet in many ways and for many days.
I have experimented and dominated in the bedroom.

Where shall I hide my face?
I am not ashamed of my actions, right or wrong; they were my choices.
I am not of less value or quality compared to virgins.
I could run a successful career because of it.
I am not unable to raise a good child because of it.

As a child, when I asked the needed questions, don't shout me down (one way or the other, I will get my answers).
As a girl, when I want the needed advice, don't shame me (the wrong mouth may talk and the wrong ears may hear).
As a woman, when I get the needed items, don't condemn me (it is not your business in any way).

I NEED TO BE ALONE

The best sound in the world is silence.
The absence of any other person's presence,
No children playing, running, or walking.
No parents ordering, condemning, or demanding.
There is an unnerving feeling when many are near.
But like an ocean after a storm, my spirit is at peace
when all alone.

The suffocating air of constant family outings, daily
activities,
The never-ending responsibility of relationships,
The constant black hole of reliving a routine of shared
time,
The compromised decisions and family-accepted
sacrifice,
The weight of blood connections and emotional
relationships is heavy.

The red threads of life have held me captive in evil
thoughts that never leave me.
Only when I am completely alone that the voices
stop.
Like a wild bird in a cage, I become every day.
How long do you think I can be kept in your shackle
before I lose all value to the word 'sanity'?

Set me free of the bonds of blood relations.
Loosen the chains you have tied before I break it beyond repair.
I need my constant time of isolation.
If not, the barely living feelings of gratitude will give way.
And there will be destruction and lamentation with any hope of resolution.

CHILD MARRIAGE

I witnessed a sin being celebrated today.
A wedding is not only allowed by law, but by any religion or tradition.

The bride was bathed in makeup to add age to her face.
Her breast has not yet been the size of an apple.
Her hips have not formed.
Her smallish body could not reach my waist yet.
Her wedding outfit carried her.
The heavy makeup could not add life to her emotionless expression.
The girl's childish features were lost to defeat and hopelessness.

But the ear-deafening music was like a whisper to the silent pleading on her mother's face.
Her other family members' eyes were blinded by the showers of dollars thrown at them by the groom's family.

A man whose youngest grandchild seemed older than his bride.
A man whose eyes watched the lifeless bride on the chair with lust.

The look he gave her made her feel violated, yet the shamelessness of his intention was shocking at the eagerness of his love for his wife.

Then the despaired mother's face changed; there is a strange look of acceptance and defeat on her face.
She walked to her daughter calmly; they shared a bitter smile as they hugged.
I looked away "God help them both"

The sound "Bang! Bang!! Bang!!!" was enough to stop everyone in their tracks.
The sound of screaming and running was what called my attention.
Then, I rushed to the location of focus to see the three bodies.
The groom, the smiling bride, and her smiling mother, all shot in the heart.

No matter what many may think, this story was one of the few with a somewhat happy ending.

THE CYCLE OF OUR LOVE

You have played various parts in my life.

You were first a stranger.
I saw you, you saw me.

You were then a classmate,
You seemed interesting enough.

You were then a friend.
We connected immediately over our love for movies.

You were my best friend.
It felt like we could read each other's minds.

You were then my lover.
I was your first love and you mine.

You were suddenly just my partner in the name.
You were my responsibility and the appearance had to
be kept.

You were just my friend,
We said it was for the best.

You were just someone I knew.

I must confess that I changed more than you did.
You, to a different shade of the same color,
Me, to the same shade of a different color.

You are now just a stranger.
I will never regret the love we shared; it helped in making us the people we are today and I hope you feel the same.

AN ODE TO PRIDE AND PREJUDICE

A timeless book.
Jane Austen is an author that is without compare
ahead of her time.
A woman after my own heart in the creative world.

Pride and Prejudice is an artwork that, no matter what,
is beautiful in all its forms.
Even the faults are to be commended.
A story of love can be relatable, no matter your race,
gender, generation, religion, or culture.
A book that entertains you, questions you and
educates you.

The words are precise and effective without video or
audio support.
The characters carry the vices and the vultures.
The applications of the themes and tones were
wonderful.
All its siblings were also good and hardly lacking in
anything.
But pride and prejudice, the original book is truly a
treasure.

If only they could see things the way we do.
Others may live in one world,
We are inhibitors in many worlds.
We are reporters of news yet to be known.
We are the inventors of things yet to be done.
We are the mouthpiece of creatures hidden in the shadow of non-existence.
We see beyond what is, to what could be.
We are creators of alternate reality and destroyers of small worlds.
We write, draw, carve, paint, weave, build and sow things from the world of imagination to the world you see.

Who are we?
We are artists and creators of the unimaginable.

SOCIETY PRESSURE

Funny creatures, we humans are, aren't we?
We struggle for freedom of some sort all our lives.
Yet we are the ones that cage ourselves at the same time.

Society has been known to have a say in every aspect of our thought.
What will society say?
How will we live in society?
This is what society accepts from you, from us.
It is funny how the pressure of people you don't know or don't even like weighs on your mind daily.

Society is the true magnitude of the statement "misery likes company".
Rules made ages ago,
Implemented by people filled with envy, bitterness, or anger.
Why can't others see the irrationality behind it?

Society is meant to unite us, and guide us, but not charge us.

GUILTY PLEASURE

What is your guilty pleasure?
That thing that you hate how much you love it.
Those things that tell you,
Those things that shame you.

What is it?
Too much of a good thing?
Or just something completely bad?

Is it a person or a thing?
Come on, say it out loud.
Is it the usual ones?
Food, video games, TV, sex, drugs, smoking, or drinking?
Or do you like a little kink in your pleasures?
Tell me, I would never tell.

There, that's better.
Did you enjoy saying it out loud to me?
How well did you feel just thinking about it?
Can you stop it?
Do you want to want it?
How guilty do you feel right now?

Think long and hard about that.

WRITER'S BLOCK

There comes a time in a writer's life when there are no words to write.
No inspiration to motivate you.
The head seems empty and the heart is restless.

For some, it is a down period.
For others, it is the time to rest.
For me, it is a challenge to break my bonds and transfer to the new world, to invade and learn from.

The period where the film in your mind stops playing,
And the words don't make the scene.
This is the fair share of many writers and some publishers.
This is writer's block.

And I have suppressed it today as I write this minute before the start of the new year, 2021.

THE BUSINESS OF RELIGION

Why has the religion of the people become a business?
Why are some churches, places of purchase?
Why have men of God become salespeople?

Why have some religious leaders considered the blessing of the Lord for sale?
Why has the devotion of many become a tool for a few people's selfish agendas?

Some religious figures brainwash worshipers into heartless weapons against each other.
Sometimes for money or material items.
Sometimes for sinful activities.

No religion should teach killing or hate.
Neither should it be an instrument of political power.

WHERE IS THE PRIDE IN BEING BLACK?

Oh, Africans, why did you choose to remain captives of the whites?
You still try to become like them.
You copy their ways,
You want their lives.

You are like a man who leaves his farm to care for another; just because you prefer the soil.
You refused to develop what is yours; hence you beg for what is theirs.
The selfish leaders all sold the people again to the oppressors and colonizers.

Honestly, have you truly and completely gained independence?
Because the time then and now, although very different, are the very same.

Our food products are given away for the benefit of leaders,
Who are still too blinded by their greed to see their foolishness?

We are still seen to be inferior to them, although this is not true.

So why do we still chase after their shining things? While we pay tooth and nail for scrapes from the table whose food came from us?

Where is your pride in your race, and where is your pride in your abilities and products?
Where is your pride in yourself?
Where is your pride in being black?

HER PERFECT DEPRESSED LIFE

The day-after-day routine,
The day-by-day smiles and fake laughs.
They would never notice the faults in her acts.
The night-after-night routine,
The night-by-night crying and panicking.
She will always be a smart, rich perfect young lady.

She will go to the right parties,
She will have the right friends,
She will date the right boys,
She will be the right balance of beauty and brains.
At least in public.

Her parents spent a fortune to keep their image.
The secret prescriptions, the private therapy sessions,
Her life is a constant out-of-body experience.
The sadness, the anger, and the paranoia were the alternatives to the numbness.
She hated her life in all its aspects,
Her rich shallow conversations and discussions.

But this is her life, no matter how depressing it may be.

No matter how her life ends, it must end.
As she lived as the pretty, smart rich perfect young lady.

DEAR BULLY

Oh, foolish human, today was the worst day to target me.
Others would have given you a warning.
But I have wrestled with my demons and they have won.
The punishments of my failure were meant to be mine alone to bear.
But they seem to have taken an interest in you.

You are in their hands.
So as the scent of your blood in the boy's bathroom,
So as the screams overshadow the sound of the crushing of bones,
So as the taste of my spit and pee mingle with your blood in your mouth,
So as the conflicting feeling of iron on your flesh clashes with the sound of my finger in your face.

Remember that no matter how many eyes see this scene or ears hear about our story,
For me excuses can be made; they will be made for me.
That way others will keep their pathetic sanity
Make no mistake, I will not be caught. I made sure of that.
Even in death, you will remain the bully in the story.

RULER OF MY HEART

Oh, my lover, my capturer,
You have claimed me, in every way possible.
I breathe only by your grace,
I crave the stings of the bruises you give me.
What a sweet pleasure I experience when your finger
digs through old wounds and rubs salt in them.

Hit me, punish me, violate me, surprise me, please, I
beg.
I am but a tool for your use.

Oh, my lover, my oppressor,
You have stolen my sanity and I was quite sensible.
The only joy I get is when I see your glorious face.
I will know no peace if from your torment I am set
free.
What amazing satisfaction do I enjoy when your
wickedness shows evidence on every inch of my body;
scars and marks fill them.

Fill me, pet me, explore me, invade me.
I need it as much as you do.

DEAR MOTHER

You deserve to live your life.
Don't sacrifice yourself for others.
All the responsibility is always going to be awaiting you.

You cannot prevent all evil from your child.
You will win some and lose some.
Your life should not revolve around us alone.

You need to be strong and become a dynamic all-around woman, you are what you want to be and not where you should be.
You can never disappoint me.
I am proud of you, my superhero.

From the daughter given to her mother.

MY DEAR FRIEND

The friendship I seek I may not find.
Many will judge it,
Some will doubt it,
Few will envy it,
But most will not understand it.

My friendship will be compared to no other
relationship I will have.
It will not be tied to the laws of society.
It will not be classified by blood or marriage.
It will recognize no gender.
It will never be twisted by time and location.
It will have no rules or regulations.
It will be pure and raw.
It will be a connection of souls and hearts.

My friend will always be my friend.
A friendship that might never be.
If this my friend truly is,
I plead God, let us meet.

THE BLACK HOLE

I fell into a black hole.
There I am in constant hunger.
For food,
For love,
For anything and everything.

First, I want something sweet,
Now, I want something sour,
Next, I want something bland,
Then I want something spicy.
My belly might be full but my mind is not.

I want something to read,
I want something to watch,
I want something to create,
I want something to listen to,
I want something to wear,
I want something to learn,
I want something to hold.

The desire is never-ending.
The satisfaction is ever fleeting.

All things shiny and new,
All things that cost a penny or more than a few.

Be it my need for a distraction,
Or a short calm for my daily frustration.

I see, I like,
I want, I buy,
I play, I am okay,
I put it away.
It starts again.

PAINT THE NIGHT

I want to paint the night today.
Not with fantasies of hope and victories or nightmares
of fears and losses,
But with colors from nature.
All mixed yet standing on their own.

Getting my inspiration from the voices of the day
before.
With the wind and clouds as my paintbrush,
Helping me to touch the endless nothingness of the
dark.

I want to bare myself to her,
Only then will she hide her secrets in my most sacred
places.
I hope that she will finally trace back the history of
my confusion.
So, I will paint paintings of emotions.

THE WAY WE ARE

Dear Friend,
I see the little hearts in your eyes.
They are love advances.
So, when you show them, I will turn blind.
So, when you speak them, I will turn deaf.

I employ you, let us not play the game of lovers, for
your spirit I will break.
Like a moth to a flame,
Like a fly to the grave,
That will be your fate.

I need to win.
This does not allow me to see till the murder has taken
place.
I just awake to the destruction I have caused.

So, I am saving you from being causative of a battle in
a war with no winners.
For the sake of the love we share, let's remain friends.
Let's stay the way we are right now.

THE LOVER'S GOODBYE

The last time I saw you,
My heart was in total denial.
My mind was blank,
My body was trembling.
That's how I knew this time was the last.

Our love was still strong,
But we were now different people.
And before love turned to hate,
Before we reached a point of no return,
No matter how sad it may be,
Different paths we had to take.

HER JOURNEY FROM FEAR TO FREEDOM

There was a baby girl, who was curious and adventurous.
She had a mother, who was always filled with regret and fear.
She had a father, who was always governing and controlling.
She had a childhood filled with broken promises and ironies.

"She was born, she survived and she died" was the story they wrote for her.
"She was seen, she was heard and she lived" was never in the books for her.

They cut off her wings and wondered why she could not fly.
They pulled out her eyes and wondered why she could not see.
They pulled out her tongue and wondered why she could not talk.
They cut off her ears and wondered why she could not hear.

"Fear, I must confess, I am not the one still holding on between the two of us"
"Fear, I must confess, most of my life I struggled with this question, to live or to die?", but not anymore.

She knelt in prayer till she got new ears
Then she listened and knelt till she got a new tongue.
Then she praised, worshiped, listened, and knelt till she got new eyes.
Then she watched, praised, worshiped, listened, and knelt till she got new wings.
Then she flew, watched, praised, worshiped, listened but no longer knelt because her feet never touched the ground again.

She has left you, fear, and gone to freedom, who has always been a better companion anyways.

FOOD ORGASM

The aroma of hot air fills the room.
The sizzling can be heard from a mile away.
The tingling of my skin intensifies as the cool breeze
kisses me.
My eyes are filled with desire as the colors fight for
my attention.
Yet, all my mind cares about is the taste.

The love they say has many faces.
Pleasure, they say can be gotten from many places.
The burning sensation many times I crave,
I finish up my meal without leaving any traces.

The sweetness of chocolate in its purest form,
The spiciness of Cameroon pepper in soaked hot
noodles,
The softness of hot Amala combined with Ewedu,
The thickness of hard-fried yam.

I cook, I serve and then I eat.
These words I write with full enthusiasm,
Many might read with full sarcasm.

I don't need a partner, just myself to have a food
orgasm.

ABOUT THE AUTHOR

Oluwabukunola Akinsanya is a B.SC graduate of Mass Communication from Pan-Atlantic University. She enjoys writing novels, poems and short stories. She is an avid reader and loves watching crime and law shows. Her favorite colors are purple and pink.

Oluwabukunola idols Jane Austen, the best-selling author of the book Pride and Prejudice. The movie Pride and Prejudice 2005 happens to be her favorite. She enjoys spending time with children and hopes to study Child Psychology at some point in her life.

Oluwabukunola loves art and has been lucky enough in life to learn and practice various forms of art like painting, drawing, tie and dye, batik and many others. She loves nature and plants.

Her hobbies include listening to music, meditating, planting and writing quotations.